What Will You Be?

by Lee Ling

Table of Contents

What Can You Be?

This boy likes to take care of cats and dogs. He likes to feed and pet them. When the boy grows up, he may want to be a vet.

⊙ This boy and his dog are good friends.

⬆ This vet helps a sick pet get better.

A vet is a doctor who takes care of animals. A vet makes sure an animal feels good.

This girl ⟳ reads every day.

This girl likes to read. Her favorite books have lots of pages. When she grows up, she may want to be an author.

An author writes books for people to read. Some authors write books just for children.

⬆ This author reads along with a young reader.

This boy likes to help his dad cook. He likes to watch people on TV cook. When he grows up, he may want to be a chef.

⊙ This boy cracks an egg over a bowl.

⬆ This chef made a wonderful meal.

A chef may run the kitchen of a restaurant. A chef may cook for lots of people.

What Else Can You Do?

This girl likes to plan and make buildings. She uses all kinds of blocks. When she grows up, she may want to be an architect.

⟲ This girl uses rubber blocks to build.

⬆ This architect has plans and a model.

An architect draws and designs buildings. Architects make sure that the buildings they design are safe.

This boy likes to put money in his piggy bank. Then he likes to count the money. When he grows up, he may want to work in a bank.

⬆ This boy likes to sort and count money.

⊕ This banker answers people's questions about money.

A banker helps people take care of their money. A banker talks about saving money.

This girl likes to take long rides on airplanes. She likes to look at the world from up high. When she grows up, she may want to be a pilot.

⬇ This girl likes to travel to faraway places.

⬆ This pilot flies many people at one time on this plane.

A pilot flies a plane. A pilot tries to give people a safe, smooth ride.

Look at this chart.
There are so many things you
could be when you grow up.

Dentist

Doctor

Police Officer

Firefighter

Teacher

Storekeeper

Now pretend that you are grown up. What are you doing?

Comprehension Check

Retell

Look back at the pictures in this book. Use them to tell a partner what you learned about different jobs.

Think and Compare

1. What do you think you need to do before you can be a vet?

2. Which jobs in this book interest you? Why?

3. How do people decide what they want to be when they grow up?